THE NON-COOKBOOK FOR THE NON-COOK

THE NON-COOKBOOK FOR THE NON-COOK

by Sandy Eshbaugh St. Clair
and Lizzie Eshbaugh Bushma

Workman Publishing
New York

Library of Congress Cataloging in Publication Data

St. Clair, Sandy Eshbaugh.
    The non-cookbook for the non-cook.

    1. Cookery—Anecdotes, facetiae, satire, etc.
I. Bushma, Lizzie Eshbaugh.
II. Title.
PN6231. C624S7 1984   818'.5402   83-40540
ISBN 0-89480-667-X

Workman Publishing Company, Inc.
1 West 39 Street
New York, New York 10018
Manufactured in the United States of America
First printing May 1982
Second printing April 1984

10 9 8 7 6 5 4 3 2 1

Dedication

To my mother... who never taught me how to cook because she was too busy teaching me how to laugh....

To my sister... who went to the store to buy lettuce and baking potatoes and came home with cabbage and red potatoes!

And to every delightful non-cook who has ever been intimidated by a * C.S.

* (Cooking Snob)

Bon appetite!

OFFICIAL NON-COOK
MEMBERSHIP CARD

Name _____

Address _____

Favorite Restaurant _____

Lifetime Member

A COOKBOOK FOR PEOPLE WHO CAN'T—AND DON'T WANT TO!

Do the words "from scratch" make you break out in hives?

Do you ever crave a peanut butter and jelly sandwich on a day when you're supposed to act grown up and eat quiche?

Have you ever failed miserably at making jello with fruit?

Do you hide your extensive list of carry-out phone numbers behind the cookbooks your friends gave you for Christmas?

If you answered YES to any of these questions, RELAX! You are a NON-COOK and you are among friends. A non-cook is a friendly, good-natured soul who for a variety of reasons does not cook. Some of us have tried and met with disaster. Some of us have friends and relatives who have intimidated us into submission. And many of us think that other things such as war, religion, politics, and children with chicken pox are more important than stuffing mushrooms or pouring liquor on bananas and setting them on fire.

This NON-COOK COOKBOOK was written especially for our fellow non-cooks who fear simple culinary tasks and who spend more time in the frozen foods section of the grocery store than they do in their own kitchens. We hope you will use it in good humor. In a country with more cookbooks than people, we finally have a cookbook we can call our own.

Happy Non-Cooking!

Sandy and Lizzie

Glossary

This glossary was written as an aid for fellow non-cooks. I hope it will help you decode the endless kitchen gibberish we face each day. Please know that on any given day I can't spell or pronounce many of these words, and when I am forced to use them in conversation they are never spoken above a whisper.

À la carte (pronounced ah lah kahrt): To order thus is to choose from a whole list dish by dish, rather than ordering from a set combination. French. ALL FAST-FOOD RESTAURANTS ARE À LA CARTE...

Bisque: Bisque is really soup. They look alike. They taste alike. They smell alike. So WHEN does SOUP become a BISQUE?! Will someone *please* let us in on the secret!

Citrus Peeler: Used mainly as a chisel for removing brown dried ketchup from the top of the ketchup bottle.

Cuisinart: If you have one of these items, please TURN IN YOUR NON-COOKBOOK. If you can also spell and pronounce this term, you're not in the non-cook class.

Glossary

Electric fruit drier: A non-cook never dries out fruit intentionally. By *accident,* well, that's a different matter! I've found that an old tin breadbox left in the sun will do the trick nicely. I've also had equal success with a forgotten bowl of fruit left above the refrigerator.

Flambé: To cover food with brandy, cognac, a liqueur; then light and serve flaming. I often FLAMBÉ my hamburgers on the grill. Sometimes we have over-flambéd steaks, depending on the wind and the amount of lighter fluid.

Melon Baller: An ice cream scoop for the dieting non-cook.

Purée: Most cooks use a blender to purée foods until they are soft and runny and sickening. Non-cooks have expanded this technique to include the *garbage disposal.* We "purée" kitchen dishrags, bars of soap, sponges, steel-wool soap pads, an occasional wooden spoon, car keys, barrettes, rubber bands, and short shish-ka-bob skewers.

Slotted Spoon: Used to uncover your remaining kitchen utensils that are buried in your kids' sandbox. Always try to remember to retrieve them in the fall, as this spoon is not quite as effective in frozen sand.

Glossary

Tongs: A MUST when cleaning out the bottom of the vegetable drawer in the refrigerator. A decomposed three-month-old tomato that you would never want to touch is removed effortlessly with tongs.

Waffle Iron: A true non-cook buys a toaster instead. It is too difficult to match the grooves in the frozen waffles with the grooves in the waffle iron.

Whisk: If you think this is only a popular laundry detergent—good for you! You are eligible for the non-cook HALL OF FAME.

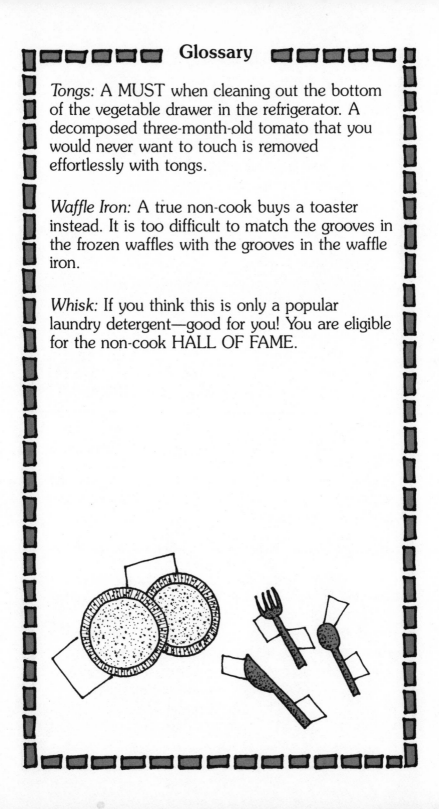

The Cook/Non-Cook Identification Chart

THE COOK	THE NON-COOK
• Makes sun tea on her back porch.	• Sits on her porch swing and drinks instant tea.
• Complains about the firmness of vegetables at salad bars.	• Feels like she's *cooking* each time she enjoys a salad bar.
• Adds wine to everything.	• Takes a unique approach to the use of wine. She DRINKS it!
• Buys a separate jar or pan for each food known to man. (Sun tea jar, omelet pan, wok, au gratin pan, soufflé pan, charlotte pan, and on and on.)	• Believes with all her heart that one jar fits all! (Leftover potato salad, instant tea, bacon drippings, and during the summer the kids store bugs in it.)
• Collects fruitcake recipes.	• Recognizes that there is only one fruitcake, which is wrapped in cellophane and circulates the country. (Have you ever seen anyone EAT a fruitcake?)

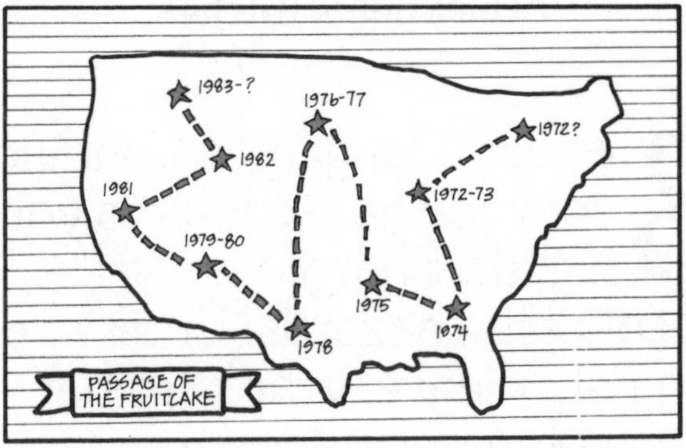
1983-?
1976-77
1972?
1982
1981
1972-73
1979-80
1975
1974
1978
PASSAGE OF THE FRUITCAKE

THE COOK	THE NON-COOK
• Working conditions: hot, greasy, messy; long hours, hazardous utensils.	• Working conditions: relaxing, friendly, neat, clean; approved by the American Restaurant Association and the Board of Health.
• Income distribution: writes a check for $168 for the privilege of carrying home 8 sacks of groceries, unloading the car, preparing dinner, and doing the dishes.	• Income distribution: pays an adorable waiter $15 for a restful hour of good food and uninterrupted conversation.
• Great hostess!	• Fantastic guest! (Where would all those good cooks be without us?)

The Cook's Kitchen

Beware! Dangerous conditions could be hazardous to your health. Sharp utensils! Potential fire hazards! Enter at your own risk! Please wear hard hat when standing under pans.

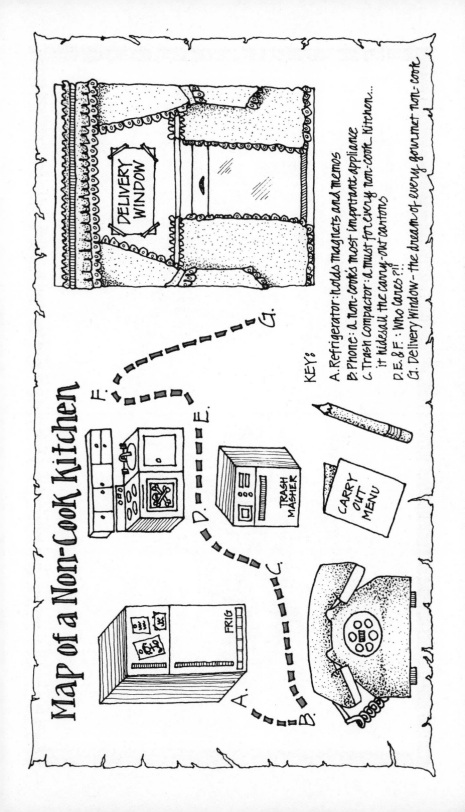

Map of a Non-Cook Kitchen

DELIVERY WINDOW

TRASH MASHER

FRIG

CARRY OUT MENU

KEY:
A. Refrigerator: holds magnets and memos
B. Phone: A non-cook's most important appliance
C. Trash Compactor: A must for every non-cook kitchen...
   It hides all the carry-out cartons
D, E. & F.: Who cares?!!
G. Delivery Window — the dream of every gourmet non-cook

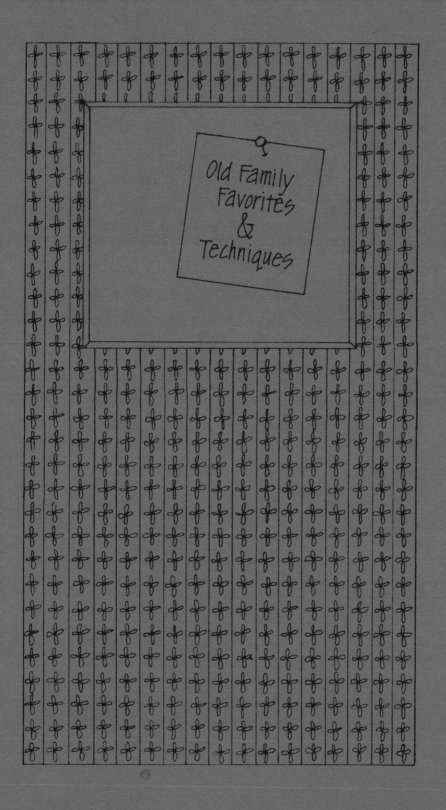

Old Family
Favorites
&
Techniques

The Non-Cook 4 Basic Food Groups

I CAFFEINE

II ALCOHOL

III SUGAR

IV SALT

This is *not* a simple task. Even a veteran chef can experience a headache brought on by this seemingly innocent little box of crystals. Be forewarned: when they say HOT water, they are talking HOT. You will know that your HOT was not the same as their HOT when those little crystals do not dissolve.

DISSOLVE, then, is the real key to success. The term DISSOLVE means every single, teeny-tiny one of those itsy-bitsy crystals must melt into the HOT water. (A lesser woman would crack under the strain!)

Next, turn your faucet on COLD and let the water run until frost forms on the stainless steel. This will meet the requirement for COLD water.

The final challenge comes when you must try to determine the precise moment to add the fruit to the jello. Try to think of it as George Washington crossing the Delaware. The element of surprise is extremely important to your success. If you add the fruit too soon, it will glide swiftly to the bottom. If you hesitate too long, the fruit will stay on the top. There is exactly a 1-to-3-second time span when your attack will succeed.

Good Luck!

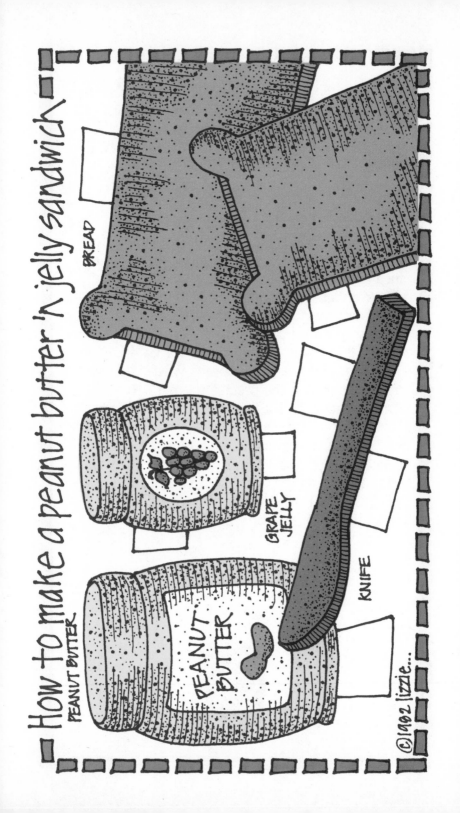

How to make a peanut butter 'n jelly sandwich

PEANUT BUTTER

BREAD

GRAPE JELLY

PEANUT BUTTER

KNIFE

©1992 lizzie...

Directions

Peanut butter and jelly sandwiches truly make life worth living. Unfortunately, they are often misunderstood... and to make matters worse, they are discriminated against on the basis of age. We are literally forced by society to outgrow our love for peanut butter and jelly. We are cultivated to crave and adore that creamy sensation as children, then, along with all the other traumas that occur as we stumble into adulthood, we are expected to give up our peanut butter and jelly... COLD TURKEY! Some people never recover. Others of us go into the "closet" and try to cope with the ache and rejection of living a lie. We go out to lunch and read the same quiche menus, dreaming of the day we can say with dignity: "I'll have the peanut butter and jelly on soft white bread, please." Until that glorious day arrives, I have taken the following steps to help ease the pain:

1. I have initiated in Scott County, Iowa, on February 20, 1984, a class action suit on behalf of the peanut butter, jelly and bread combination for age discrimination violations.

2. I have filed a request for a legal name change from "peanut butter and jelly" to "crème de la peanuts avec concord pâté" to be used on all official documents when referring to said sandwich.

3. A P.B.J.S. Hotline has been set up for those in need of a sympathetic ear... Just call: 1-800-586-6000.

Keep the faith!

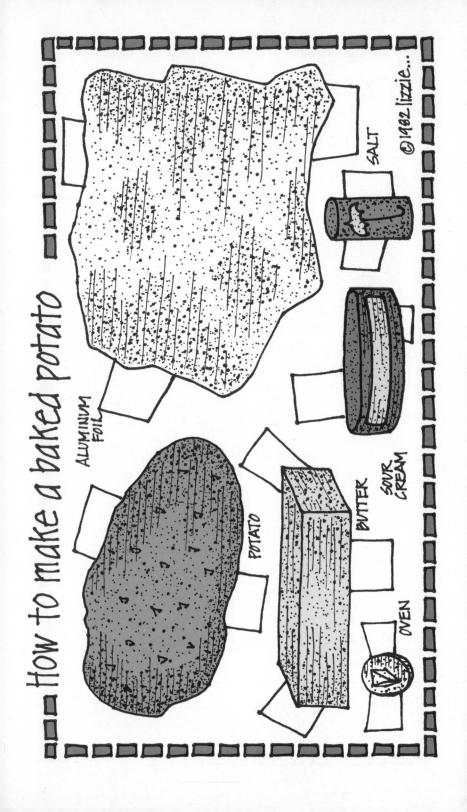

Potatoes should be brown, but not too brown. Upon close inspection you will notice that some of the brown is indeed dirt. Therefore, you must develop a keen eye to determine the difference between brown and BROWN!

Furthermore, brown potatoes very often have small white bumps on them. When the bumps begin to elongate, you have your basic "root formation." Now, if this root is long enough for you to grab firmly, chances are good that you have a rotten potato at the other end. You can verify your suspicions by squeezing said potato gently between your thumb and forefinger. If you now swear that you are holding a raw oyster, you are most definitely the proud owner of one totally worthless potato.

Please commit the following to memory:

Soft before baking: very *suspicious*!
Soft after baking: simply *delicious*!

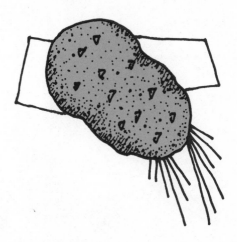

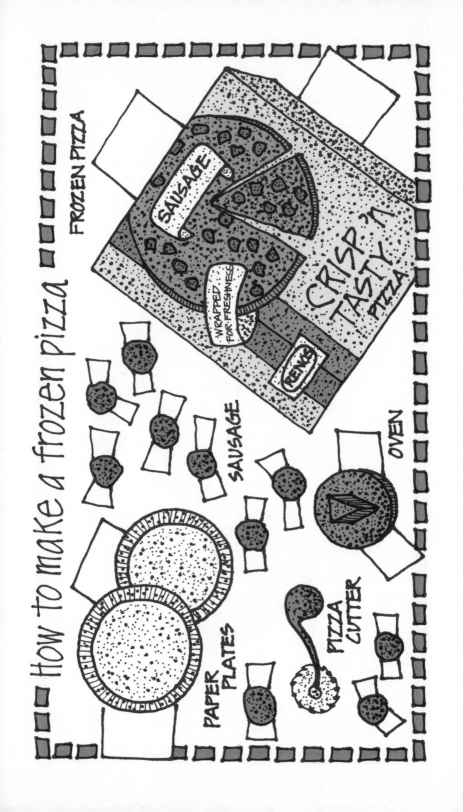

How to make a frozen pizza

FROZEN PIZZA

SAUSAGE

WRAPPED FOR FRESHNESS

CRISP 'N TASTY PIZZA

REINS

SAUSAGE

OVEN

PAPER PLATES

PIZZA CUTTER

"Never take a frozen pizza for granted."
—Anonymous

When you are face to face with a frozen pizza, please give it your undivided attention. Do not, under any circumstances, crumple up the cellophane wrapper before you read the printed cooking instructions. The wonderful folks who have spent countless hours preparing your pizza have done so with specific instructions in mind. They would be *disgusted* to know that after all their hard work and dedication you botched up the final product. So give some thought to the man who spent eight hours a day shredding that mozzarella cheese so evenly. Give some thought to the woman on the third shift who chopped the green peppers for you. Your pizza is a part of their very lives... give it all the attention and care it deserves!

Attach to your refrigerator...

SAVE THE
CELLOPHANE!

How to make chocolate chip cookies

BOX OF CHOCOLATE CHIP COOKIE MIX

CHOCOLATE CHIP COOKIES

OVEN

CHOCOLATE CHIPS

Grandpa's CHOCOLATE CHIP COOKIE MIX

The thing I hate most about cooking snobs is the terms they use. Take the phrase "from scratch," for example. Every C.S. in the world will let you know that her baked goods are "from scratch." Now, I don't care how you slice it, "SCRATCH" is an ugly word. When I think of "SCRATCH" I picture cats, mosquitoes, and small red bumps and blotches all over my skin. When I add the word "FROM" I start to imagine where the "SCRATCH" came "FROM." Well, let me just say that it can be a most unappetizing thought. It is for this reason that I never, and I must emphasize *never*, make a heavenly food like chocolate chip cookies from "SCRATCH." There is absolutely nothing scratchy about the way those wonderful morsels melt on your tongue . . . and furthermore, I never have to worry about where they came "FROM" . . .

THEY COME FROM A *BOX* AND DON'T EVER FORGET IT!!

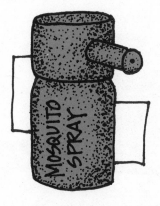

How to make newlywed soup

TOASTING GLASSES

Bride   Groom

CAN OF SOUP

Campbell's CONDENSED Chicken with Rice SOUP

HEARTS

"How do I love thee... Let me count the ways!"

So what if COOKING is not one of the ways? I'd like to verbally abuse the person who said, "The way to a man's heart is through his stomach." I polled 857 grooms on their wedding day and not one of them was even hungry!

Newlywed Soup is a sentimental favorite for the loving couple who never confuse their hearts with their stomachs. The soup is a delicate blend of chicken and rice that flows tenderly from its red-and-white can, carefully designed to remind one of Valentine's Day. And the symbolism of the chicken and rice reminds you of the first night of your honeymoon. The white rice that was in your hair, your shoes, your suitcase. A jealous bridesmaid threw some so hard that it stung your face. What could possibly be more appropriate for Newlywed Soup than rice? So you see, the perfect newlywed meal is indeed Chicken with Rice soup. Just add candlelight and soft music.

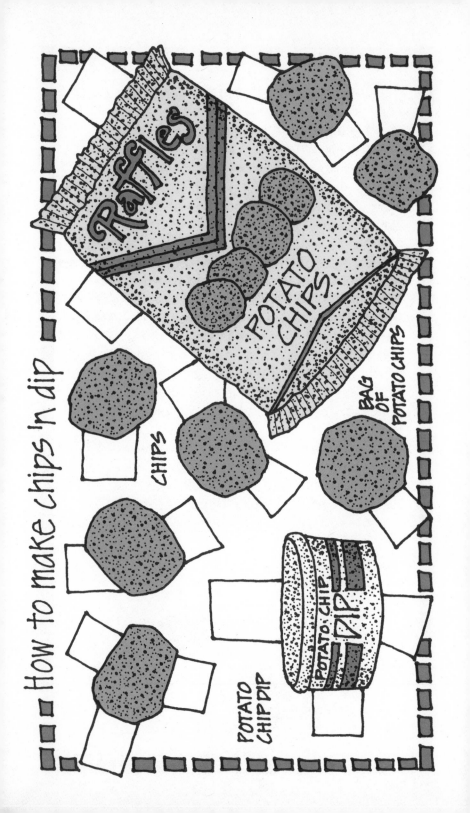

◼◼◼◼◼ Directions ◼◼◼◼◼◼

This morning I tipped the scale at a delicate 128 pounds. When I checked into marriage as a blushing bride, I was at a fighting weight of 110 pounds. There are, therefore, exactly 18 additional pounds of *me* floating around. I realized that 10 of those pounds had been added in the last six months, making this dubious accomplishment rather astounding. I've examined carefully all the keys to my weight gain success and decided that it was the natural result of CHIPS AND DIP... Yes, your ordinary household "chips and dip" will do the trick nicely. If you would like to duplicate my success, you will find the following steps helpful:

1. Always open a fresh bag of chips for yourself when you are alone and allow it to "breathe" for at least 5 minutes, like a fine red wine.

2. Make sure the dip has been chilled to 45°F.

3. Stir the dip with your forefinger and your first chip... carefully blending all ingredients.

4. Be sure to dip at least 1 teaspoon of dip per chip...

Now enjoy!

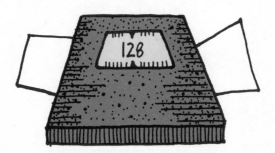

How to make frozen fish sticks

BOX OF FROZEN FISH STICKS

Mrs. Pal's
CRISPIER CRUNCHIER
16 FISH STICKS
NET WT 12OZ

SPATULA

FISH STICKS

Mrs. Pal's
TarTer sauce

TARTER SAUCE

COOKIE SHEET

The delicate aroma of frozen fish sticks baking sends me on a sentimental journey. It must be similar to the way John-Boy feels when he returns to Walton's Mountain. I can see my mother opening that green-and-white cardboard package. I can hear the THUD-THUD-THUD as the frozen fish hits the tin cookie sheet. She always put the fish sticks on the bottom shelf of the oven and the frozen French fries on the top shelf. Then we would all gather around and watch her add 2 tablespoons of mayonnaise to the tartar sauce package...Oh, could that woman make tartar sauce! Sometimes we would break into song; other times we would just hold hands around the table and compose lengthy prayers. We were truly grateful...

Goodnight John-Boy
Goodnight Mary Ellen
Goodnight Jim-Bob

How to make canned green beans

GREEN BEANS

PAN

HAND CAN OPENER

CAN OF GREEN BEANS

BUTTER

© 1982 lizzie...

Directions

Canned goods are always full of surprises. I feel a surge, a spirit of adventure... an anxiety, each and every time I sink my can opener into that fresh tin. Green beans are a personal favorite. I've always admired the clever way they put those cute little pictures on the front of the can — just to throw you off the track. People can't wait to discover whether the beans in the can are as green as the ones on the label. It's thrilling! In some remote parts of the country it's second only to the Fourth of July fireworks. I've known women who couldn't stop opening those cans. Entire families stand around the kitchen counter to "ooo-ahh" at the array of green that springs forth when the lid is lifted. Yes, green beans are destined to be the greatest thing since cracker jack prizes!

So happy opening...

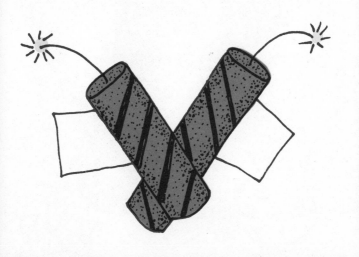

How to make an ice-cream sundae

MARSHMALLOW TOPPING

BUTTERSCOTCH TOPPING

CHOCOLATE TOPPING

©1982 lizzie....

CHERRY

SUNDAE CUP

STRAWBERRY

CHOCOLATE

NUTS

VANILLA

SPOON

NUTS

"I never met an ice cream sundae I didn't like."
—Anonymous

In my humble opinion, ice cream sundaes are the answer to world peace. This is such a simple solution that I'm amazed no one has come up with it before.

FACT: It is impossible to eat an ice cream sundae and feel hostile.

FACT: Ice cream sundaes come in such varieties that every taste bud around the world could be satisfied.

SOLUTION: Proclaim a moment in time when every person on earth would simultaneously eat an ice cream sundae.

Sure, we'd have our problems coordinating it all—but it's workable! We'd need to allow for refrigeration problems near the equator—monsoons—tornadoes—and of course we'd need to avoid any scheduling that might conflict with viewing *General Hospital* and *All My Children*. Obviously, some people would need to get up in the middle of the night to participate. I for one would be willing to make such a sacrifice for the good of all mankind. I sincerely believe that we could move the Secretary of State to a new office in a Baskin-Robbins store and set this entire program in motion in no time.

Write your congressman today!

How to make a "democratic" dinner party

PAPER PLATES

PAPER NAPKINS

PAPER CUPS

PLASTIC SILVERWARE

CENTERPIECE

FLAGS

The Fourth of July is the official day of the NON-COOK DINNER PARTY. Non-cooks across the nation repay all previous invitations on this one glorious day. A non-cook dinner party is a "democratic" dinner party. Do not think of this as a Fourth of July POTLUCK, but rather as a celebration in keeping with the ideals and principles of our democracy.

As a perfect non-cook hostess you do not cook one thing. You do provide paper plates, cups and napkins, and plastic "silverware." You also provide one red, white and blue tablecloth, an appropriate centerpiece, and an abundance of drink.

To plan the menu, simply phone the guests. Appeal to their cooking ego: "Blanche, nobody in this town makes potato salad like you do. If I tried for weeks, I'd never be able to do what you do for that salad. You could bring some?! Oh, WONDERFUL! Everyone will just love it!" Invite as many people as it takes to fill your table with food. When the menu is settled, spend the rest of the day decorating with cute little American flags or taking a nap.

As your food-carrying guests arrive, you will encounter an interesting phenomenon. Each cook has done her best to outcook the competition. Your table will resemble the cooking booth at the state fair. The dishes will take on first names. Alice's coleslaw...Joan's artichoke salad. But here's the best news of all: in a few months, people will only remember they had a marvelous meal at your house. They'll completely forget it was a "democratic" dinner party...

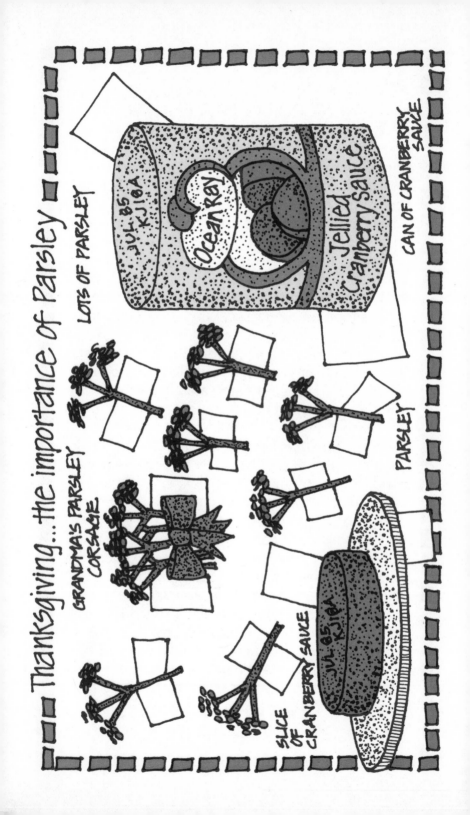

Thanksgiving...the importance of Parsley

LOTS OF PARSLEY

Ocean Ray

Jellied Cranberry Sauce

JUL 85 KJIOA

CAN OF CRANBERRY SAUCE

GRANDMA'S PARSLEY CORSAGE

PARSLEY

SLICE OF CRANBERRY SAUCE

JUL 85 KJIOA

Holiday Shortcuts

We always knew it was Thanksgiving, because that was the only day of the year when Mom bought PARSLEY and CANNED CRANBERRY SAUCE. She would come home from the store with one bushel of parsley and six cans of jellied cranberry. (There were six of us.) Mom believed that the best defense against her questionable cooking talents was to have a great offense— and her offense was parsley! First she would place a delicate sprig of parsley behind her ear to put her in the mood. Then she would grab a large bowl and create the parsley Thanksgiving centerpiece. Next she would weave the traditional parsley napkin rings. While Dad put the turkey in the oven and peeled the potatoes, Mom would carefully wash the remaining parsley and fashion bouquets for each dish. Some years when she wasn't rushed for time, Mom would make a parsley corsage for Grandma.

Finally, it came time to unmold the cranberry sauce. Dad would make the gravy while Mom did the most amazing thing. She would open those cans and slide the cranberry mold out in ONE UNBROKEN PIECE! Every year we could count on reading the serial number on the bottom. (Mom says it's all in the wrist.)

Ah, traditions.

How to make Christmas fudge

BOX OF CANDY STORE FUDGE

NANNY FAY

YUMMY FUDGE

DULL KNIFE

CUTE CHRISTMAS BASKET

The Christmas season is a particularly stressful time for the true non-cook. One of my neighbors is a girl scout leader, a boy scout leader, a Sunday school teacher, and an aerobic dance instructor. Every December 20th she delivers a basket of assorted baked goods with foreign names to my door. The sugar in her voice combined with the sugar in her basket puts me into a diabetic coma. When I'm finally revived, I realize that I am now expected to show my holiday spirit by producing a basket of goodies. This fudge recipe was devised to get me through such a crisis:

1. Buy two pounds of fudge at a reputable candy store. (I never said this was economical.)

2. Buy an adorable basket with the appropriate Christmas ribbon.

3. Place the fudge in your own 9 x 11 Pyrex dish. Put it in a warm oven and watch it until it starts to melt.

4. Remove the warm fudge from the oven and recut it with an old knife. Make it sloppy. If you have a three-year-old child in the house, let him cut the fudge.

5. Arrange the warm fudge in the basket.

6. You are now ready to deliver the fudge. Practice this next part several times in front of a mirror, using exactly the following phrase:

"MERRY CHRISTMAS... SORRY THE FUDGE IS SUCH A MESS, BUT IT WAS STILL HOT WHEN I CUT IT."

Official Non-Cook Weights, Measures and Equivalents...

1 cup
equals...
¼ large empty
mayonnaise jar

½ cup
equals...
empty tuna can
filled to rim

4 tablespoons
of butter
equals...
size of Milky Way
candy bar

1 teaspoon
equals...
1½ Pepsi
Bottle Caps...
(Remove the
cork lining
to insure accurate
measurements.)

(Based on the standard U.S. Metric Fluid Volume)

Emergency Substitutions

To the non-cook emergency substitutions are a natural part of everyday life. A state of emergency usually sets in at about 4:30 P.M. At this time we must face the nagging question: "What should I fix for dinner?" This daily crisis makes our hearts pound faster, increases our pulse rate, and leaves us gasping. We consider this our substitution for jogging.

Some of us have also experienced brilliant moments of highly creative and divergent thinking to cope with this condition. I've included several of my own brainstorms. Take time, at about 4:30 today, to start your own emergency substitution file. Trade your substitution ideas with a non-cook who doesn't get home until 4:45 P.M. We're all in this mess together!

Emergency Substitutions

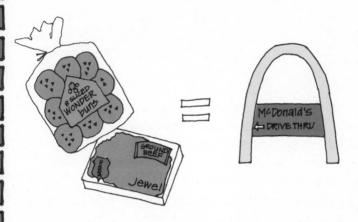

One pound ground
beef, one package
sesame seed buns

equals...

one quick trip
through the
drive-up window!

Fresh-grated
coconut

equals...

the inside of a
mounds candy bar
(Carefully nibble
away the dark
chocolate coating...
it's a dirty job,
but somebody's
got to do it!)

Emergency Substitutions

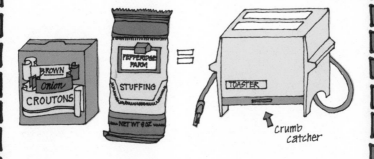

Croutons, stuffing   equals...   the crumb tray
or bread crumbs   of your toaster.

Sifted all-purpose   equals...   one 15-minute
   flour, whole   trip to the bakery.
wheat flour, active
    dry yeast

Emergency Substitutions

_____

_____

_____

_____

_____

_____

_____

_____

_____

_____

_____

_____

_____

_____

Restaurant,
Carry-Out, &
Friends who
Cook

The Dinner Dilemma: An Etiquette Guide for the Non-Cook

A non-cook has three options when deciding how or where to dine: restaurant reservations, carry-out (pick-up or delivery), or inviting yourself to a friend's house for dinner.

White-glove publications have long ignored the finer points of non-cook dinner options. I have always considered these books to be rude, and this simply proves my point! I am proud to say that we non-cooks now have our own etiquette guide.

RESTAURANT RESERVATIONS

• Keep all restaurant phone numbers on a laminated card in your wallet, next to your driver's license.

• Be flexible and cheerful when calling for your reservation. Assure the person at the other end that any cooking is better than yours and you're looking forward to a terrific meal.

CARRY-OUT (PICK-UP OR DELIVERY)

• Keep these numbers by the phone, listed right under Police, Fire Department, and Ambulance.

• Get on a first-name basis with the person taking the phone orders. When they know you, they don't put you on hold and they include extra pickles with your order.

INVITING YOURSELF TO A
FRIEND'S HOUSE FOR DINNER

(This is admittedly a tacky approach, but nonetheless a viable option when you are a true non-cook and you are hungry.)

• Keep a card file in your recipe box with the names and dinner hours of all your friends.

• Get dressed up and stand at their front door. Let your stomach growl until they hear it and ask you in!

Eat your heart out, Emily Post!

NON-COOK NUTRITION WHEEL

FORD

monday ☐ **Carry-Out** ☐ tuesday ☐ wednesday ☐ thursday ☐ friday ☐ saturday ☐ sunday ☐ monday ☐

☐ saturday ☐ sunday ☐ monday ☐ tuesday ☐ wednesday ☐ tuesday ☐

☐ wednesday ☐ thursday ☐ friday ☐

□ monday □ **Carry-Out** □ tuesday □

_____

_____

_____

_____

_____

_____

_____

_____

_____

_____

_____

_____

_____

_____

To the Glory of Restaurants

I love restaurants.

I love everything about restaurants.

I love their smell.

I love all those friendly people whose job it is to serve me food.

I love the music on their AM-FM radios.

I love the sound of clinking dishes and the chatter of people enjoying themselves.

I love the dim lights and those cute little glasses with candles in them.

I love those perfect little squares of butter wrapped in silver paper.

I even love those plastic flowers.

Every time I see a restaurant being built, I pause—and reflect—and thank heaven I'm not the only one who loves restaurants.

Restaurants

♡ hot dogs ♡ ♡ hot dogs ♡

(decorative border: "hot dogs ♡" repeated around all four edges of the page)

_____

_____

_____

_____

_____

_____

_____

_____

_____

_____

_____

_____

Restaurants

hot dogs ♡ ♡ hot dogs

(decorative "hot dogs ♡" text repeated along all four margins)

_____

_____

_____

_____

_____

_____

_____

_____

_____

_____

_____

_____

_____

_____

The Joy of Catching a Cooking Snob at a Fast-Food Restaurant

Life can be joyful! The first wedding of your thirty-four-year-old sister is a time of joy. The pregnancy of your thin aerobics teacher is also a time of joy. But let's talk BLISS. Bliss is catching a cooking snob at the counter of a fast-food restaurant with her two children who only have wholewheat and sprout sandwiches in their lunch boxes.

Your first impulse will be to shout, "You've been caught, you fraud!" I suggest, however, a more indirect approach so you can savor the moment. This next line is a great conversation starter. Feel free to use it with my blessing.

"Hello there. I've heard the beef on the bun is really quite good this time of year."

Ninety-three percent of all cooking snobs will respond in the following way: (The other 7 percent are still hiding in the restrooms.)

•They will always give you an elaborate excuse on why they are there—"This is the only restaurant within a five-mile radius of my child's Suzuki violin instructor, and the instructor forbids them to take a lesson on an empty stomach due to an ancient oriental custom."

•They will squint and pretend not to be familiar with the menu.

•They will give the darling high school boy very specific cooking instructions with their order.

•They will devour everything on their tray.

•They will pretend not to know where the garbage can is.

Friends Who Cook

Friends Who Cook

Poultry,
Eggs, Men,
Etc.

The Non-Cook's Guide to the Produce Department

The produce department of a supermarket poses the supreme challenge to the non-cook. We are at home in the frozen foods and canned goods sections because those friendly, colorful boxes and cans tell us exactly what to do with the food inside. We have some comfort in the meat department because we are able to talk to those incredibly charming butchers. But in the produce department it is every woman for herself!

The following guide was developed to aid the non-cook. You won't be an expert on selecting the best fruits and vegetables, but I guarantee you will look like one!

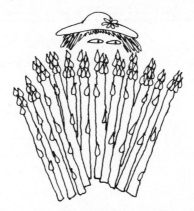

THE SQUEEZING GROUP

Lettuce	Lemons	Oranges
Pears	Limes	Grapefruits
Apples	Cauliflower	Mangoes
Avocados	Nectarines	

THE SHAKING GROUP

Melons   Coconuts   Watermelons
                                            (bring a
                                            strong friend)

THE PINCHING GROUP

Grapes   Tomatoes   Green beans
(watch out for   Broccoli
flying seeds)

THE CARESSING GROUP

Cucumbers   Quince   Kiwis
Bananas   Green peppers   Rutabaga
Papayas   Eggplant

THE DO-NOT-TOUCH GROUP

Ugly fruit   Includes artichokes, bean
(the name   sprouts, pineapples.
says it all!).

Note: Don't judge a beet by its droopy leaves. Think of them as women over forty. They may have a few gray hairs, but the rest of them is in perfect cooking condition.

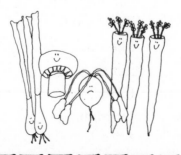

Poultry and Eggs

I've always admired courageous humans who brave the unknown. One of those unsung heroes of our past has to be the first man who decided to *eat* an *egg*. He had a dream and he followed his heart. He thought food should be more than ripping meat off the bloody bone. While other men were hunting deer, bear, and buffalo, our hero was sticking his hand under chickens. Those of us who love fluffy omelets owe him a great deal. He passed through this world but once, yet his spirit and imagination remain with us always...

The Man of Your Dreams

Getting to know the right butcher may be the most important contact of your life. The following "Guide to Getting to Know Your Butcher" was tested and proven to be an effective way to meet that handsome devil and have him unlock the mystery of red meats.

DAY 1

When you go to the grocery store, dress for the butcher. Keep in mind that he will be viewing you mainly from the waist up, and give particular attention to blouse, sweater, hair, make-up—and color. The man is surrounded by red meat and white uniforms all day long. Do not, therefore, under any circumstances, dress in red or white.

Open your closet and go for the gusto. Remember your only competition is carcasses and uniforms. You will undoubtedly be the most gorgeous creature he will see all day...so put a smile on your face, a song in your heart, and go to the supermarket.

You need to make four passes by the meat counter. Stop and study the selection, and *don't* feel intimidated by the labels. Today you are there to smile and wave to the butcher.

DAY 2

You are ready to *press the buzzer.* Remember that the buzzer only rings in the room where the butcher is cutting meat. If you are overly anxious and push the heck out of that buzzer (thinking all the while that it must be broken), you can be sure that you have sent the man *into orbit*. If the butcher doesn't appear, pick another supermarket and go back to Day 1.

If the butcher does appear, you will need something to say to him. Fear not! On the way to the meat counter, pick up a canned ham (any size, any brand). Walk to the buzzer with confidence, press it firmly *one* time, and wait patiently. When the butcher appears, ask him if he would please "shave" the ham...and make sure to tell him there is absolutely *no* hurry. Do the rest of your shopping, and when you return to pick up your "ham shavings" thank him as if he has just donated a kidney for a life-saving transplant. You now have a mountain of shaved ham and the beginning of a relationship with your very own butcher.

DAY 3

Today will be a snap—it is poultry day and there is nothing confusing about a chicken. Chickens have only a few basic parts and they are all easily identifiable. If your butcher is stocking the counter, stroll over and ask if he has any boneless, skinless chicken breasts. Casually mention that you really wanted to make Chicken Kiev for dinner, but you just don't have time to do the deboning yourself. Chances are he won't have any available, which gives you yet another opportunity to be gracious and understanding. If he does have some, you'll be stuck with one package of skinless, boneless chicken. In that case, take it home and bake it, chop it up, add some mayonnaise, and make one terrific chicken salad sandwich. The important thing is that now your butcher knows he is dealing with a *discriminating woman.*

DAY 4

You are ready for the big time—ready for *red meats.* Now, red meats are nothing to be feared . . . but they are a little tricky. The labels are usually smeared, and even when they are readable, terms like "prime," "lean," "extra-lean," and "choice" can't mean the same thing to all people. You need someone you can count on to explain the subtleties. You need *your butcher!*

Technique enters here and it is important. Hold your neatly prepared shopping list in one hand and gently caress the packages of red meat with the other. Then pick up any package that you can afford and gaze at it with a faraway look. Saunter slowly over to the buzzer and give it a delicate touch . . . still gazing. When your butcher appears, make eye contact instantly. (Eye contact is essential.) Hand him your package of meat and whisper, "What is *your* absolutely favorite way to cook this cut?" Make it personal. Remember you are dealing with a man who *loves* meat . . . he spends eight hours a day touching and chopping it, so you can be sure he knows how it should be cooked. If he is truly the prince that most butchers are, he too will begin to gaze. He will describe in great detail how to cook, serve, and chew that gorgeous red meat. Once he begins to talk with that gaze in his eyes, you will know that you have a friend. Together you have shared a "moment," and he will be someone you can count on forever . . .